THE CAMPHOR WAY

HOW TO BURN BRIGHTLY, LET GO, AND LEAVE A LASTING IMPACT

HIMANSHU SAXENA

Contents

FOREWORD

The Wisdom Hidden in Disappearance

Some philosophies tell you to be like water—flowing, adaptable, taking the shape of whatever container you are placed in. Others tell you to be like fire—burning brightly, consuming everything in your path to fuel your ambition.

But few have looked at camphor.

Camphor burns completely, leaving no trace behind. It doesn't hold on to its form, doesn't cling to its existence, yet its presence lingers long after it is gone.

This book is about that paradox—how letting go is the ultimate power.

In a world obsessed with status, validation, and self-promotion, Be Like Camphor offers a radical shift in thinking. It is not a book about chasing success, but about becoming undeniable—about creating such lasting impact that even when you are no longer present, your influence remains.

As you turn these pages, you will find wisdom from ancient Indian thought, modern philosophy, and personal insights that challenge everything you thought you knew about success, legacy, and influence.

Read it not as a book, but as a mirror. You will see yourself in its lessons. And if you let it, it may just change the way you move through the world.

PREFACE

The Story Behind This Book

A few years ago, I found myself in a conversation that changed me.

I was speaking to a mentor—a quiet man, never in the spotlight, yet deeply respected by everyone who knew him. I asked him what he thought was the secret to lasting influence.

He smiled and said, **"The strongest forces in the world are the ones you don't see. Wind. Gravity. Thought. You don't need to be visible to be powerful. You just need to be necessary."**

That idea stayed with me.

We live in a world where visibility is currency. People measure their worth by how many followers they have, how loudly they can proclaim their ideas, how much recognition they receive. But the ones who truly shape the world are rarely the ones shouting the loudest.

I began exploring this concept—reading ancient texts, studying philosophy, observing leaders who moved without seeking attention. That's when I discovered the philosophy of camphor.

This book is the result of that journey.

It is not a guide to winning in the traditional sense. It is a guide to creating, leading, and letting go without losing yourself. To burning brightly without clinging to the flame.

If you have ever struggled with feeling unseen, with the fear of letting go, or with the desire to create something that outlasts you, this book is for you.

You don't have to chase influence. You just have to be like camphor.

Acknowledgements

This book was not written alone.

To the mentors, thinkers, and quiet leaders who have shaped my understanding of these ideas—this book carries your wisdom.

To my readers—those who seek not just success, but meaning—I hope these pages offer you a new way of seeing the world.

To those who have lived the philosophy of camphor—who burn without fear, who leave behind not possessions but influence—you are the reason this book exists.

Thank you.

Prologue

The Camphor Way

In a small temple courtyard, a priest lights a piece of camphor. The white, waxy substance catches fire instantly, flickering for a few moments before vanishing into the air. No ash. No residue. Only its fragrance lingers.

It is gone, yet its presence remains.

For centuries, fire has been a symbol of transformation, water of resilience, and earth of stability. But camphor? It represents something deeper. It burns, but it does not destroy. It gives light, yet asks for nothing in return. It disappears completely, leaving behind only its essence.

Camphor is not an element, yet it holds the wisdom of them all. It teaches us how to live without clinging, to give without expectation, to influence without seeking recognition.

In a world obsessed with being seen, heard, and remembered, the way of camphor offers a radical alternative: Disappear, and let your essence do the work.

This book is not about playing small. It is about playing so well that you no longer need the spotlight. It is about finding strength in detachment, power in silence, and legacy in the lives you touch—without leaving a trace.

To be like camphor is to master the art of invisible greatness.

This is your invitation.

Are you ready to burn bright and let go?

I

The Forgotten Element – Beyond Fire, Water, Earth, Air, and Space

The Five Elements—And the One That Contains Them All

For thousands of years, we have been told that everything in existence is made of five great elements:

1. **Earth (Prithvi)** – the foundation, the steady force that holds things together.
2. **Water (Jal)** – fluidity, adaptability, resilience.
3. **Fire (Agni)** – passion, destruction, transformation.
4. **Air (Vayu)** – movement, intellect, expansion.
5. **Space (Akasha)** – vastness, emptiness, the realm of potential.

Every philosophy, every self-improvement book, every spiritual teaching finds its root in one of these elements. Be grounded like Earth. Be adaptable like Water. Be fierce like Fire. Be free like Air. Be limitless like Space.

If the five elements represent different forces, then **Camphor is the unifying force that embodies them all.**

Camphor refuses to be just one thing. It is a paradox—a substance that does not stay within the limits of any single form. It is solid, yet it disappears. It burns, yet it does not destroy. It spreads, yet it leaves nothing behind except its fragrance.

Camphor is movement between the 5-fundamental elements.

- It stands firm like Earth, yet it does not resist change.
- It dissolves like Water, yet it does not lose its essence.
- It ignites like Fire, yet it does not consume or leave ruins behind.
- It spreads like Air, yet it does not drift aimlessly.
- It disappears into Space, yet it remains present through its scent.

Camphor is the in-between state, the perfect blend of action and detachment, of presence and absence, of giving and letting go.

It does not fight between forces—it moves through them effortlessly.

This is why camphor is a way of being.

To understand camphor is to understand how to exist without attachment, how to give without loss, how to disappear yet remain unforgettable.

A New Way to See Power and Presence

Look at the way we live our lives today.

- Some people burn too hot—chasing success with relentless intensity, only to burn out (Fire).
- Some people keep adapting—never standing their ground, always adjusting to fit in (Water).
- Some people stay too rigid—afraid of change, resisting movement (Earth).
- Some people float aimlessly—chasing every new idea without direction (Air).
- Some people drift into nothingness—losing themselves in distractions and detachment (Space).

But what if you could have all of these qualities in perfect harmony? Camphor does not struggle between these forces. It knows how to be **solid**, how to flow, how to **burn**, how to **spread**, and when to **disappear**.
This is not just a lesson in nature. It is a lesson in how to live.

1. Be like Earth when you need stability. Stand firm in your principles.
2. Be like Water when you need flexibility. Adapt to challenges without losing yourself.
3. Be like Fire when you need transformation. Burn away what no longer serves you.
4. Be like Air when you need to expand. Move freely, explore, grow.
5. Be like Space when you need to let go. Detach from what holds you back.

But most importantly, be like Camphor—know how to be all of these at once.

The Strength of Those Who Leave No Trace

Society teaches us to chase permanence. Build a legacy. Make a name for yourself. Be remembered.

But camphor **does the opposite**. It burns **completely**. It doesn't leave behind ashes or residue—only fragrance.

And yet, that fragrance lingers long after the camphor itself is gone.

This is the paradox of true influence:

1. The most powerful people are not those who demand attention—but those whose presence is felt even in their absence.
2. The most successful people are not those who cling to power—but those who give themselves fully and then let go.
3. The most fulfilling life is not one where you chase recognition—but one where your impact outlives your need for validation.

Camphor is the ultimate teacher of selfless impact.
It does not seek to remain, yet it is never forgotten.
It does not cling to itself, yet it gives fully.
It does not fight to exist, yet its essence lingers everywhere.
This is the philosophy of being like camphor.

- Not to hold on, but to give freely.
- Not to chase recognition, but to let your essence do the work.
- Not to be bound by a single element, but to embody them all.

What This Book Will Teach You

The five elements represent different aspects of life, but camphor shows us how to move between them effortlessly.

This book is not about telling you to be like fire or be like water.

It is about teaching you how to be everything at once—how to balance intensity and calm, attachment and detachment, presence and absence.

To live fully, without clinging.
To create impact, without obsession.
To let go, without losing meaning.

Because the ones who change the world are not those who burn out, or those who endlessly adapt, or those who hold on too tightly.

The ones who change the world are like camphor.

They disappear—but their presence is never forgotten.

Coming Up Next:

Camphor Burns, Yet Leaves Nothing Behind – A Lesson in True Impact
Why the greatest things we do are often the ones no one sees.

II

Camphor Burns, Yet Leaves Nothing Behind – A Lesson in True Impact

The Myth of Lasting Impact

We all want to matter.

We want our work to be remembered, our names to be spoken long after we're gone. So, we build, we chase, we hustle—convinced that true success is about leaving a mark so deep that the world can't forget us.

But here's the harsh truth: the world forgets.

Look around. How many great artists, writers, and leaders have been buried by time? How many once-famous entrepreneurs now exist only as footnotes?

Even the biggest legacies eventually fade.

Buildings collapse. Companies get acquired. Books go out of print. Statues erode.

So, if everything is temporary, what kind of impact should we really aim for?

Camphor holds the answer.

The Strength of Burning Completely

If you've ever seen camphor burn, you know it doesn't leave behind ashes. Unlike wood, which burns and turns to dust, or metal, which melts and hardens again, camphor disappears completely.

No residue. No remnants. Only a lingering fragrance that stays long after it's gone.

This is the highest form of impact—not one that leaves ruins behind, but one that leaves an essence.

It's easy to mistake visibility for influence. We assume the loudest voices are the most powerful, the ones who leave their names etched in history are the ones who mattered most.

But look at the world's greatest teachers, mentors, and innovators. Their real gift wasn't in making sure they were remembered. It was in creating something that continued to shape the world, even when their names were forgotten.

Steve Jobs didn't need his name on every Apple product—his vision is in every iPhone.

The best teachers don't create followers—they create leaders who go on to surpass them.

The most influential people are those who build things that outlive them—not just in name, but in function.

Camphor doesn't burn for itself. It burns to transform everything around it.

Imagine applying that philosophy to your life.

The Power of Disappearing: Why Ego is the Greatest Trap

Ego is the voice that whispers:
"Make sure they know you did this."
"Make sure they remember your name."
"Make sure you get credit."

It's the reason people slap their names on buildings, fight over job titles, or spend more time curating their personal brand than actually doing meaningful work.

But the more you seek recognition, the less real impact you make.

Think about the most effective people in your life.

The mentor who changed the way you think, even if you don't remember their name.

The friend who gave you advice years ago, and it still shapes your decisions.

The book that rewired your brain, even if the author isn't famous.

These people didn't work for credit—they worked for change.

The best leaders, teachers, and creators don't obsess over their personal legacy. They focus on building something so powerful that it keeps going, even when they step away.

What This Looks Like in Real Life

? The Founder Who Walks Away

The best entrepreneurs don't cling to their companies forever. They build systems that can thrive without them. They don't need to hold onto power. They burn bright, then move on—leaving behind something that runs without them.

? The Artist Who Lets Go

A true artist doesn't create for applause. They create because they have something to give. The greatest works aren't the ones that shout the loudest—they're the ones that slip into people's hearts and shape them silently.

? The Mentor Who Doesn't Need Recognition

The most powerful teachers aren't the ones who hoard knowledge and demand gratitude. They give freely, knowing their success isn't in how many people admire them—it's in how many people grow because of them.

Ego seeks credit.

Camphor seeks change.

One is exhausting. The other is freedom.

Leaving a Fragrance, Not a Scar

Camphor doesn't fight to remain. It doesn't burn for attention. It doesn't leave behind ruins.

Yet, it's never forgotten.

It lingers in the air, invisible but present.

That's the kind of impact worth aiming for—not one that demands recognition, but one that changes things in a way that is felt, even when we are gone.

Work in a way that the results remain, even if no one remembers who did it.

Lead in a way that your absence is not a disruption, but proof of your success.

Live in a way that your influence is real, even if your name fades.

This is the camphor way.

Because in the end, it is not about how long we stay visible, but about what remains when we are gone.

Coming Up Next:

The Power of Disappearing: Why Ego is the Greatest Trap
The more we seek credit, the less influence we actually have.

III

The Power of Disappearing – Why Ego is the Greatest Trap

Would You Still Do It If No One Knew?

Let's start with a question that might make you uncomfortable.

If you worked hard on something—a business, a book, an idea, a piece of art—but no one ever knew you created it... would you still do it?

Most people wouldn't.

Because, deep down, we don't just want to do great things. We want people to see them. We want appreciation, recognition, proof that our existence mattered.

And that's where ego traps us.

We measure our success not by the impact of our work, but by how many people notice it.

We confuse visibility with influence.

We mistake applause for value.

Camphor teaches us something radical:

? True influence is silent.

? The most powerful forces in life don't seek attention—they simply transform everything around them.

Why the Loudest People Often Have the Least Power

Look at the people who desperately crave attention. The ones who interrupt in meetings just to sound smart. The ones who chase clout instead of mastery. The ones who build for personal success, not real impact.

They may get noticed, but they rarely get respected.

Now look at the people who actually shape the world.

1. The leader who doesn't micromanage but empowers.
2. The writer whose ideas spread, even if their name fades.
3. The mentor who gives knowledge freely, expecting nothing in return.

They don't waste energy seeking credit.

And because of that, they actually earn it.

Ego says: "Make sure people remember you."

Camphor says: "Do the work. Let the fragrance linger."

One fights for attention.

The other is effortless.

The Paradox of Real Power

The people who try the hardest to be influential often become forgettable.

Think about history.

The names we remember aren't always the ones who built the biggest monuments to themselves.

They're the ones whose **ideas became so natural, so universal, that we forget they ever had an origin.**

The wheel.

The alphabet.

The first person to teach a child numbers.

No one remembers the inventor of fire.

Yet fire changed everything.

True power isn't about being seen.

It's about becoming essential—so much so that your influence spreads without your name attached to it.

How Ego Kills Your Potential

Ego convinces you that your success is about you. That you need to be celebrated. That your work isn't valuable unless it comes with recognition.

But the moment you need recognition, you give away your power.

- The artist who stops creating because they're not getting enough likes? Trapped.
- The employee who works only for promotions, not for mastery? Trapped.
- The leader who can't step away because they need to be the hero? Trapped.

When your work depends on external validation, you're no longer doing it for yourself. You're doing it for applause. And applause fades.

Camphor doesn't burn for recognition.

It burns because that's its purpose.

What if you worked the same way?

How to Apply This in Your Life

? Work for mastery, not for approval.

Forget job titles, external praise, and validation. Instead, focus on getting so good that results speak for themselves.

? Detach from credit.

Let go of the need to be the face of every project. The most respected people are those who quietly make things happen.

? Give without expectation.

The people who give freely—knowledge, ideas, support—become invaluable. The ones who hoard? Easily replaced.

? Ask yourself: "Would I still do this if no one knew?"

If the answer is no, check your intentions. Are you doing this for impact or for recognition?

True Influence Is Invisible

The irony of ego is that the more you chase recognition, the less lasting your impact becomes.

Camphor burns completely—leaving no residue, no proof it was ever there. But its fragrance lingers.

That's the kind of power worth having.

1. Be the leader whose presence isn't about control, but about the strength of what they leave behind.
2. Be the creator whose work shapes minds, even if no one remembers their name.
3. Be the kind of person whose influence doesn't need credit to exist.

That's how you become unforgettable—by not needing to be.

Coming Up Next:

Give Without Attachment – The Secret of Effortless Influence
How to contribute without seeking validation.

IV
Give Without Attachment – The Secret of Effortless Influence

Think again. Would You Really Do It If No One Knew?

Let's say you gave someone a life-changing opportunity—maybe you recommended them for a job, mentored them, or helped them through a rough time.

And then they moved on. No acknowledgment. No gratitude. No "thank you for everything."

Would you still do it?

Most people wouldn't. Not because they don't want to help, but because they expect something in return—at least recognition.

That's where most of us get it wrong.

We think giving is about exchange. A favor for a favor. A kind act for appreciation. Work for validation.

But camphor doesn't work that way.

Camphor burns completely, giving light and fragrance, and then it vanishes. No residue. No ashes. No sign that it was ever there.

And yet, its presence lingers.

Now imagine what your life would look like if you gave without keeping score.

What if you could help, contribute, create—not because you need recognition, but because it's just who you are?

This isn't about being selfless to a fault. It's about something bigger:

Giving without attachment.

Acting without expecting a return.

Being free from the exhausting need for approval.

Because the moment you do that, you become truly powerful.

The Need for Credit Is a Weakness

Look at the people who desperately chase validation.

1. The ones who constantly remind everyone how much they've done.
2. The ones who expect loyalty as a reward for their generosity.
3. The ones who feel bitter when their contributions go unnoticed.

Now look at the ones who give freely, effortlessly.

1. They don't cling to past favors.
2. They don't need to be seen as important.
3. They move forward without resentment.

Which one seems lighter? Freer? Happier?

The first group gives to control. The second gives to grow.

And people can always tell the difference.

The Paradox of True Influence

The more you try to own your impact, the weaker it becomes.

Look at the greatest thinkers, teachers, and creators. Their work is everywhere, yet their names aren't always attached to it.

- No one remembers who invented the wheel.
- No one remembers the first person to tell a story.
- No one remembers the first teacher who taught numbers to a child.

But their influence? Everywhere.

Because true giving isn't about proving your worth—it's about making things better, whether or not anyone gives you credit.

Camphor burns without hesitation, and because of that, its fragrance lingers.

What if you could do the same?

How to Give Without Attachment

1?? Detach from Recognition
Give because it aligns with who you are, not because you want something back.

2?? Stop Keeping Score
You're not a bank. If you help someone, don't track what they owe you.

3?? Do Work That Speaks for Itself
The best way to get recognized? Stop seeking it. Do such good work that people can't ignore it.

4?? Give Without Control
Once you've helped someone, let it go. Their response is not your responsibility.

5?? Trust That It Will Come Back in Unexpected Ways
Karma isn't about instant returns. It's about long-term patterns. Give freely, and the universe will return it—just not always from where you expect.

True Giving Leaves No Residue—Only Influence

Camphor doesn't wait for applause. It doesn't care if anyone notices.

And yet, long after it's gone, its fragrance remains.

That's how real impact works.

Not by forcing things to happen.

Not by expecting something in return.

But by giving freely and letting go.

This is the camphor way.

Because the less you need from others, the more they want to give back.

Coming Up Next:

Purity in Thought, Action, and Intent – The Power of Clarity in Decision-Making and Relationships

V

Purity in Thought, Action, and Intent The Power of Clarity in Decision-Making and Relationships

Are You Saying What You Mean?

Have you ever said "yes" when you wanted to say "no"?

Have you ever smiled at someone you disliked?

Have you ever done something just because it looked good, even though it didn't feel right?

If you have, don't worry—you're not alone. We all do it. Society teaches us to be polite, agreeable, and strategic.

- We say things we don't mean to avoid conflict.
- We take actions that don't align with our values because they bring approval.
- We pretend our intentions are pure when, deep down, we know there's something else driving us.

And this creates an invisible tension inside us. We're not at peace—not because the world is hard, but because we are misaligned with ourselves.

Camphor doesn't have this problem.

It burns completely—no hesitation, no residue, no hidden intent. It doesn't try to be something it's not. It doesn't care how it looks. It simply does what it is meant to do.

Imagine if you could live that way.

- No overthinking.
- No second-guessing.
- No pretending.

Just pure thought, pure action, pure intent.

That's what clarity looks like. And once you have it, life gets a whole lot easier.

Why Most People Are Stuck

Most people live with a constant background noise of doubt, anxiety, and second-guessing.

Not because life is complicated. But because they are out of sync with themselves.

They:

- Think one thing but say another.
- Say one thing but do another.
- Do things without even knowing why they're doing them.

And this creates mental clutter.

- Every time you say yes when you want to say no, you add another layer of stress.
- Every time you hide your true feelings, you dilute your own voice.
- Every time you do something just to fit in, you lose a little piece of who you are.

Until one day, you look in the mirror and realize... you don't even know what you truly want anymore.

That's what happens when you live in a state of misalignment.

Camphor doesn't struggle with this. It knows exactly what it is. It burns freely, without contradiction.

And that's what you need to do too.

The Three Levels of Clarity

To get rid of this invisible mental weight, you need to purify three things:

1?? Purity in Thought

Your mind is the source of everything. If your thoughts are chaotic, your actions will be chaotic.

If you secretly hate your job but force yourself to "be grateful," you'll feel drained.

If you envy someone but pretend to be happy for them, that resentment will eat at you.

If you constantly suppress your real opinions, you'll eventually lose confidence in your own voice.

The fix? Brutal honesty with yourself.

Don't suppress uncomfortable thoughts—acknowledge them. See them clearly. Then decide how to deal with them.

2?? Purity in Action

Your actions should match what you truly believe.

Don't fake excitement for things you don't care about.

Don't force yourself to do things that don't align with who you are.

Don't try to "appear" a certain way just to impress people.

Act with integrity. Not in the moral sense, but in the sense of being whole, undivided.

What you do should be a reflection of what you truly think and believe.

3?? Purity in Intent

Intent is where most people struggle.

A lot of stress comes from doing things with hidden motives.

Helping someone, but secretly expecting them to help you back.

Being kind, but only because you don't want to upset anyone.

Working hard, but not because you love what you do—just because you want external validation.

When your intent is unclear, everything feels like a transaction. Every interaction feels loaded. Every relationship feels like a balancing act.

But when your intent is pure—when you give freely, when you act honestly, when you say what you mean—everything becomes effortless.

And ironically, people trust you more when they can sense that your actions don't come with strings attached.

How to Apply This in Your Life

✓ In Work: Stop over-explaining. Say what you need. Set clear boundaries. Be direct.

✓ In Relationships: Stop playing games. Be honest about what you want. Say no when you mean no.

✓ In Creativity: Stop chasing trends. Create what actually excites you.

✓ In Decision-Making: Choose based on what feels true to you, not what looks good to others.

The moment you stop pretending, manipulating, and overthinking, everything gets easier.

Pure Action = Effortless Confidence

When your thoughts, actions, and intent are aligned, you don't second-guess yourself.

? You say no without guilt.

? You say yes without hesitation.

? You move through life without mental clutter.

Camphor doesn't hesitate before burning. It doesn't worry about how it looks or whether it will be appreciated. It just does what it's meant to do.

And because of that, its presence lingers long after it's gone.

That's the power of clarity.

Coming Up Next:

The Beauty of Detachment – How to Let Go Without Losing Yourself

VI

The Beauty of Detachment – How to Let Go Without Losing Yourself

If You Lost Everything Tomorrow, Who Would You Be?

Imagine this.

You wake up one morning, and everything you've built—your job, your reputation, your relationships—is gone.

No LinkedIn title. No status. No people recognizing you for your work.

Who are you without it?

Most people would spiral. Because for most of us, our identity is tangled up in what we own, what we achieve, and how others see us.

We mistake attachment for meaning and possession for purpose.

- We hold onto titles and careers like they define our worth.
- We hold onto relationships, even the broken ones, because we fear being alone.
- We hold onto the past, wishing things had gone differently.
- We hold onto expectations for the future, constantly worrying about what's next.

And what do we get in return? Anxiety. Exhaustion. Fear.

We don't own our attachments—they own us.

Now look at camphor.

Camphor burns completely—without hesitation, without fear. It doesn't cling to its form. It doesn't resist its own transformation. And yet, it leaves behind its essence.

That's real detachment. Not apathy. Not numbness. Not indifference.

Just the freedom to exist fully, give completely, and then let go—without fear.

What if you could live that way?

Detachment Isn't Indifference—It's Freedom

Most people confuse detachment with not caring.

They think letting go means becoming cold, distant, or withdrawn.

They think freedom means walking away from responsibility.

They think a peaceful mind means not feeling anything deeply.

But real detachment isn't about running away—it's about showing up fully, completely, and freely.

You can love someone deeply without clinging.

You can be ambitious without being obsessed with success.

You can create meaningful work without being controlled by praise or criticism.

Detachment means you are fully engaged in life, but not imprisoned by it.

You own your work, your relationships, and your ambitions—but they don't own you.

Letting Go at Work: Detachment Isn't Passivity

Let's clear something up—detachment doesn't mean staying silent about your work. It doesn't mean you shouldn't ask for a raise, take credit for your achievements, or advocate for yourself.

It means you do these things without tying your self-worth to the outcome.

Here's what detachment at work looks like:

? Attachment:

Seeking validation for every task you complete.

Feeling crushed when someone else gets credit.

Letting rejection shake your confidence.

? Detachment:

Doing great work because it's who you are, not because you need constant applause.

Sharing your achievements with confidence, but not desperation.

Asking for what you deserve, but not falling apart if things don't go your way.

When you detach, you don't stop caring—you just stop being controlled by the need for recognition.

And ironically, detached people often get MORE recognition.

Why? Because they're not constantly seeking it.

They're too busy doing work that speaks for itself.

Why Letting Go Makes You More Powerful

If you're attached to something, it controls you.

If you attach your happiness to money, you'll always feel insecure—because no amount will ever feel like enough.

If you attach your identity to your job, any setback will feel like a personal failure.

If you attach your worth to a relationship, you'll be terrified of losing it.

But the moment you let go, you become free.

You don't stop working—you just stop obsessing.

You don't stop loving—you just stop clinging.

You don't stop striving—you just stop suffering.

Camphor doesn't resist burning. It doesn't hold back. It gives fully and then lets go.

And because of that, its presence lingers long after it's gone.

That's real power.

How to Practice Detachment in Everyday Life

1?? At Work: Do Your Best, But Don't Be Defined by Results

Ask for the raise, pitch the idea, share your wins—but don't attach your self-worth to whether you get the outcome you want.

Build a reputation, not an identity. Your work is what you do, not who you are.

2?? In Relationships: Love Without Control

You don't "own" people. Let them be who they are.
Love freely, but if someone leaves, let them go with grace.

3?? With Success: Enjoy It, But Don't Fear Losing It

If you win, great. If you fail, great. Both will pass.
Focus on the process, not just the reward.

4?? With Emotions: Feel Deeply, But Don't Get Stuck

Pain, sadness, anger—they're temporary.
Let them pass through you, instead of gripping onto them.

5?? With the Past & Future: Stay Here

Stop replaying past mistakes.
Stop obsessing over the future.
The only thing real is this moment—live in it fully.

Detachment = Inner Peace

When your happiness is not dependent on external things, you become unshakable.
? You can walk into any room with confidence—because your worth isn't tied to approval.
? You can speak your truth—because you don't fear rejection.
? You can take risks—because failure doesn't define you.
This is what it means to be like camphor.
To give everything.
To exist fully.
To let go when the time comes.
Because only those who are willing to let go can experience true freedom.

Coming Up Next:

Why Silent Work is the Most Powerful Work – The Art of Achieving Without Self-Promotion

VII

Why Silent Work is the Most Powerful Work – The Art of Achieving Without Self-Promotion

If You Had to Stop Talking About Your Work, Would It Still Be Recognized?

Imagine two people working at the same job.

The first one constantly talks about everything they do. Every minor achievement is turned into a performance—carefully crafted to be seen, liked, and shared. They spend more time promoting their work than actually doing it.

The second one keeps their head down and works. They focus on the craft itself, not the applause. They don't rush to prove themselves—they let their results do the talking.

Now ask yourself: Who do you think will last longer?

The answer is obvious. Substance always outlasts noise.

The people who shout about their work might get noticed first. But over time, their value depends on how much they can keep performing. The moment they stop talking, they disappear.

But the people who focus on doing great work, regardless of whether anyone is watching?

They become irreplaceable.

Because real power isn't in how much attention you can get. It's in how undeniable your work becomes.

Why People Fear Silent Work

Most people don't want to work in silence.

Because silence means:

No instant validation.

No external motivation.

No guarantee that people will notice.

And that's terrifying.

We've been trained to believe that if we don't constantly remind the world of our worth, we'll be forgotten.

That if we don't post about our progress, it doesn't count.

That if we don't network aggressively, we'll be left behind.

That if we don't build a "personal brand," we'll fade into irrelevance.

So we overcompensate.

We start caring more about being seen as productive than actually being productive.

We crave visibility so much that we mistake attention for achievement.

But camphor teaches us a different kind of power.

It burns completely, giving off light and fragrance, and then disappears. It doesn't demand recognition. It doesn't need to be seen to be felt.

And yet, its presence lingers.

That's how silent work operates.

The Power of Being So Good, You Can't Be Ignored

Here's the hard truth: The best work doesn't need promotion. It speaks for itself.

Think about the greatest writers, inventors, and artists.

Many of them weren't viral sensations when they were creating. They weren't spending all their time marketing themselves. They were just obsessed with the work itself.

And because of that, their work became so powerful that it couldn't be ignored.

- Steve Jobs didn't spend time trying to be famous—he focused on building things so legendary that fame came to him.
- Haruki Murakami writes novels without caring about interviews, panels, or social media—his words travel across the world without him needing to promote them.
- Some of the best coders, designers, and engineers aren't the loudest voices in the room—but they're the people everyone depends on.

Silent work is about playing the long game.

It's about trusting that if your work is truly valuable, it will create its own momentum.

You won't need to force it.

But Don't You Need to Share Your Work?

Let's get one thing straight—this isn't about staying invisible forever.

Silent work doesn't mean you never showcase your work. It means:

✓ You focus on doing the work first before worrying about talking about it.

✓ You let results drive your reputation, not empty self-promotion.

✓ You don't seek attention—you let attention find you.

You should absolutely share your achievements. But there's a huge difference between:

? Talking about your work to seek validation.

✓ Talking about your work because it has real value to offer.

One feels desperate. The other feels effortless.

Camphor doesn't have to announce its presence. It burns, and the fragrance spreads naturally.

What if you could do the same?

How to Make Silent Work Your Superpower

? 1. Work on Your Craft More Than Your Image

Stop obsessing over visibility. Focus on being so good that people come looking for you.

? 2. Build a Reputation, Not a Performance

Don't chase credit—chase excellence.

People respect those whose work is undeniable, not those who constantly demand recognition.

? 3. Let People Discover You

Instead of forcing yourself into every conversation, let your impact do the talking.

The most valuable people in any room are the ones whose presence is felt, even when they aren't trying to be noticed.

? 4. Share When It Matters, Not Out of Fear

Don't be silent out of insecurity. Speak when you have something worth saying.

When your work is great, you won't need to over-explain it.

? 5. Trust That Real Influence is Built Quietly

The best leaders, thinkers, and creators don't scream for attention.

They create things so valuable that the world finds them.

Silent Work = Unshakable Power

Imagine walking into a room and not needing to prove yourself.

Imagine working in a way where people notice you because of what you build, not because of how loudly you talk.

Imagine creating things that are so good that they carry your presence forward, even when you're not there.

That's what camphor does.

That's what silent work does.

It doesn't need to be loud.

It doesn't need to demand attention.

It becomes essential on its own.

That's the kind of success that lasts.

Coming Up Next:

Invisible, Yet Unforgettable – The Real Mark of Success

VIII

Invisible, Yet Unforgettable – The Real Mark of Success

The Most Important Person in the Room Is Usually the Least Noticeable

Think about the most powerful people you've ever met.

Not the loudest. Not the flashiest. Not the ones constantly reminding you of their accomplishments.

But the ones whose presence you felt the moment they entered a room.

They don't fight for attention.

They don't try to dominate conversations.

They don't perform.

And yet, when they speak, everyone listens.

That's real power. The kind that doesn't come from noise, but from substance. From mastery. From quiet confidence.

Most people chase visibility. They think success is about being the loudest in the room, the most followed online, the most recognized in their industry.

But the truth?

The greatest leaders, the most influential minds, the real game-changers—are often the least visible.

They don't need the spotlight. They become the light.

The Visibility Trap: Why Being Seen Isn't the Same as Being Valuable

The world tells you: Be seen. Be known. Be everywhere.

That's why people obsess over personal branding. Why they feel the urge to constantly post, promote, and prove themselves.

But there's a difference between visibility and impact.

Look around.

- Some of the smartest people in the world aren't famous.
- Some of the wealthiest people you'll never hear about.
- Some of the most powerful decision-makers aren't the ones giving speeches—they're the ones quietly shaping the outcomes.

And here's the paradox:

The more you chase recognition, the less powerful you become.

Why? Because when you need constant validation, you give away your power to others' opinions, others' approval, others' attention.

Real power is when your influence exists even when you're not in the room.

Why Loud Success Fades, But Quiet Influence Lasts

Think about the names you hear every day—trending entrepreneurs, viral influencers, people dominating the news cycle.

Now think about the names that have actually shaped the world.

They weren't always the loudest.

They weren't always on stage.

They weren't the ones chasing visibility.

They were the ones doing the work.

- Satoshi Nakamoto created Bitcoin and vanished. His impact? Still growing.
- Warren Buffett rarely does interviews. Yet the financial world follows his every move.

- Amancio Ortega built Zara into a fashion empire without making himself a celebrity CEO.

They mastered the art of being invisible, yet unforgettable.
Just like camphor.
It burns completely, disappears entirely—and yet, its essence lingers.

How to Become Invisible, Yet Unforgettable

1?? Focus on Mastery, Not Publicity
Be so good at what you do that people have no choice but to notice.
Recognition should be a side effect, not the goal.
2?? Lead Through Actions, Not Words
The best leaders don't micromanage or seek attention. They build systems that work even in their absence.
People respect those who create impact without demanding credit.
3?? Detach from the Need for Recognition
Stop doing things just to be seen.
Do them because they matter. Because they are worth doing.
4?? Speak Only When It Matters
When you don't talk all the time, your words carry more weight.
The most respected people aren't the ones who talk the most—they're the ones whose words shift perspectives.
5?? Trust That Influence Doesn't Need to Be Loud
The strongest forces in the universe—gravity, time, thought—are invisible.
Just because people don't see you doesn't mean they don't feel your presence.

The Camphor Legacy: Influence Without Noise

Think about the people who've shaped your life the most.
It's probably not the ones who shouted the loudest.
It's the ones whose words, actions, and wisdom stayed with you—even when they weren't around.
That's the kind of impact worth having.
Not to be the most visible.
Not to be the most followed.

But to be so essential that even when you disappear, your presence lingers.
Just like camphor.

Coming Up Next:

Influence Without Seeking Recognition – Mastering Quiet Influence and Leaving a Mark Without Making Noise

IX

Influence Without Seeking Recognition – The Art of Knowing When to Step Forward and When to Step Back

The Modern Dilemma: If You Don't Show Your Work, Do You Even Exist?

There's an old saying: If a tree falls in a forest and no one hears it, does it make a sound?

Now, here's a modern version:

If you do great work but no one knows about it, does it even count?

We live in a time where visibility is currency. Your career, your influence, even your opportunities often depend on how well you can show your work and get credit for it.

And yet, the paradox is this—the people who are obsessed with recognition often end up with less of it.

We've all seen them.

- The person who takes credit for every small thing, annoying everyone in the process.
- The colleague who is louder about their achievements than the work itself.
- The self-promoter whose reputation feels... hollow.

So, where's the balance?

How do you ensure that your work gets noticed without constantly chasing recognition?

How do you build influence without making everything about yourself?

This is where the philosophy of camphor comes in.

Camphor burns completely—it gives everything it has, and then disappears. But even after it's gone, its fragrance lingers.

That's the kind of influence you want.

You don't have to scream for attention. You just have to make yourself impossible to ignore.

Why Visibility Matters (But Only in the Right Way)

Let's be real—if no one knows what you bring to the table, you will be overlooked.

This is not ancient India where kings discovered hidden sages meditating in forests. If you stay completely silent about your work today, someone else will take the credit.

So, yes, you have to make your work visible.

But here's the mistake most people make: They focus on visibility first, and value second.

They try to be seen before they have something truly great to show.
They spend more time marketing themselves than mastering their craft.

And when that happens, their reputation is built on noise instead of depth.

The trick is to reverse the order.

First, make your work so good that it demands attention.
Then, make sure the right people see it—without overdoing it.

The 3 Laws of Smart Visibility

1?? Share, But Don't Shout

Show your work, but let the work itself be the loudest voice in the room.

Speak when there's something worth saying—don't talk just to be heard.

Think about the people in meetings who talk too much. Does anyone actually respect them? No. People respect the ones who only speak when it truly adds value.

The same rule applies to your work. Share it, but don't shove it down people's throats.

2?? Let Others Speak for You

If you're doing great work, you won't need to constantly remind people—it will naturally spread.

Instead of saying, "Look at what I did," create something that makes people say, "You have to check this out."

The best kind of recognition? When others talk about your work for you.

That's how thought leaders are built—not by constantly self-promoting, but by doing things so valuable that people can't help but share them.

3?? Take Credit Without Looking Desperate

This is where most people struggle.

You don't want to be overlooked. But you also don't want to be that guy who makes everything about themselves.

The key? Own your work with confidence, but without ego.

- When someone asks about your achievements, state them clearly—but don't over-explain.
- When you contribute to something, make sure your role is known—but don't steal the spotlight from others.
- When you succeed, acknowledge the team that helped—but don't disappear entirely from the credit.

Confidence is quiet. Insecurity is loud.

The people who command the most respect aren't the ones demanding recognition. They're the ones whose value is so clear that recognition comes naturally.

How to Apply This in Real Life

? At Work → Speak up about your contributions in a way that highlights results, not just effort. Instead of saying, "I worked really hard on this," say, "Here's the impact this project had."

? In Business → Market yourself, but don't overhype. The best brands don't need to say "We're the best"—they just prove it.

? On Social Media → Share your wins, but not in a way that sounds like you're fishing for praise. Teach, provide value, and let your expertise shine through.

? In Leadership → Lead by example, not by demanding recognition. The best leaders aren't the ones talking about leadership—they're the ones people naturally want to follow.

The Camphor Way: Influence Without the Ego

Camphor burns without hesitation. It doesn't cling to its form. It doesn't need to be seen to be felt.

Yet, even after it's gone, its presence lingers.

That's the balance.

Be visible, but don't be desperate.

Own your work, but don't let it own you.

Build a reputation, but make sure it's built on substance, not noise.

Because in the end, the people who quietly create, lead, and build are the ones who leave the most lasting impact.

And when you get that balance right?

You don't have to seek recognition. It finds you.

Coming Up Next:

The Paradox of True Power – The More You Let Go, the More You Have

X

The Paradox of True Power – The More You Let Go, the More You Have

The Empty Hand That Holds Everything

There's a scene in Kung Fu Panda 3 where Master Oogway says, "The more you take, the less you have."

At first, it makes no sense. If you take more, shouldn't you have more?

But think about it.

Try holding a handful of sand. Grip it too tightly, and it slips through your fingers.

Try clutching water. The harder you squeeze, the faster it disappears.

This is life. The things we cling to—power, money, relationships, success—are often the things we end up losing.

Yet, the paradox is this: the moment you stop grasping, you gain more than you ever imagined.

The strongest leaders don't control—they empower.

The wealthiest people aren't the ones who hoard—but the ones who invest. The happiest people aren't those who hold on desperately—but those who let go with grace.

Camphor shows us this truth. It burns away completely, never trying to preserve itself. And yet, its presence lingers.

This is real power—the kind that comes not from holding on, but from knowing when to let go.

The Illusion of Control

We spend our lives trying to control everything—our careers, our relationships, our future. We believe that if we just work hard enough, plan well enough, or push a little more, things will go exactly as we want.

But life doesn't work like that.

- The job you fought so hard for suddenly becomes meaningless.
- The relationship you tried to fix still falls apart.
- The money you saved obsessively still doesn't make you feel secure.

No matter how much you grip, some things are simply not in your hands. But what if the secret isn't in gripping harder—but in learning to let go?

The More You Let Go, The More You Have

Look at the greatest warriors in history.

A swordsman who grips his blade too tightly loses his fluidity. He becomes slow, predictable. The best fighters hold their weapon lightly—firm enough to control it, loose enough to move freely.

Life is the same way.

A leader who micromanages everything creates a suffocating workplace.

An artist obsessed with perfection never finishes their masterpiece.

A friend who is desperate for approval becomes exhausting to be around.

The irony?

When you stop clinging, you gain everything.

- When a leader trusts their team, people rise to the occasion.
- When an artist allows imperfection, creativity flows.
- When a person stops seeking validation, they become magnetic.

The moment you stop grasping for control, you create space for something even greater.

Camphor's Lesson: Burn Without Fear

Camphor burns completely, leaving no trace of itself behind. It doesn't try to resist. It doesn't hold back. It gives everything, and then disappears.

But what remains?

Its fragrance.

Its presence lingers even in its absence.

What if we lived like that?

What if we gave fully, lived boldly, and then let go—trusting that what truly matters will remain?

This is the paradox of true power.

The more you let go, the more you actually have.

How to Apply This in Real Life

? At Work: Don't try to control every detail. Delegate. Trust. Let go of micromanaging, and you'll gain respect and efficiency.

? In Relationships: Love without possession. Let people grow without needing to control them. The more space you give, the stronger the bond.

? In Creativity: Stop obsessing over perfection. Let go of fear, and you'll create more freely.

? In Life: Accept that some things are beyond control. Let go of the need to force outcomes, and you'll find peace.

True Power is Knowing When to Let Go

Look at the ocean. It doesn't hold on to its waves; it lets them rise and fall.

Look at the trees. They don't cling to their leaves; they let them go in autumn, knowing new ones will come.

Look at camphor. It doesn't try to stay; it burns, disappears, and leaves behind something even more powerful—its essence.

This is the way of life. The more we let go, the more we gain.

Because in the end, true power isn't about holding on.

It's about knowing when to release.

Coming Up Next:

Leaving a Fragrance That Stays Long After You're Gone – Why Legacy Isn't What You Own, But What You Leave Behind in Others

XI

Leaving a Fragrance That Stays Long After You're Gone

The Man Who Built No Monuments

There is a story about a man who lived in a small Indian village. He wasn't a king, a warrior, or a businessman. He never built grand temples or led armies. He didn't leave behind vast wealth or famous works of art.

And yet, long after he was gone, his presence remained.

The village children still spoke of the man who taught them under the old banyan tree, explaining the ways of the world in stories.

The farmers still used the irrigation system he designed—one that saved them from drought year after year.

The young men and women still repeated his words when making difficult decisions, remembering how he once helped them find their way.

No statues were built in his honor. No books were written about him.

Yet, in every corner of the village, in the laughter of children, in the wisdom passed from generation to generation, in the quiet resilience of those he once helped—he was still there.

This is legacy. Not the kind written in stone. But the kind written in people.

What Will You Leave Behind?

Most people think of legacy as something you own.

- A business empire.
- A fortune passed down to the next generation.
- A name carved into history.

But these things fade.
Businesses collapse. Money is spent. Names are forgotten.
True legacy isn't in what you keep.
It's in what you give away.
It's in the knowledge you share.
The lives you touch.
The values you pass down.
When you leave this world, what will remain of you?
Not your job title.
Not the number of followers you had.
Not the things you accumulated.
But the invisible impact you had on others.
Just like camphor, which disappears completely when it burns—yet leaves behind its fragrance.

The Illusion of Permanence

Look at history.
Mighty empires have crumbled.
Magnificent palaces have turned to dust.
Great kings, once feared and revered, are now nothing more than names in forgotten texts.
And yet, some things remain.
The teachings of a humble monk from centuries ago still guide millions.
A scientist's forgotten notebook leads to a breakthrough decades later.
A teacher's words, spoken in a quiet classroom, shape the life of a future leader.
The world does not remember possessions.
It remembers ideas.
It remembers kindness.

It remembers the ones who made a difference—not by trying to be remembered, but by simply giving fully.

The Camphor Way: Legacy Without Attachment

Camphor never clings to its form.
　It burns completely, vanishing without a trace.
　And yet, it is never truly gone.
　This is how true impact works.

- The best mentors don't seek gratitude. They invest in people, knowing that their lessons will live on in ways they may never see.
- The greatest artists don't chase fame. They pour their souls into their work, knowing that those who need it will find it—maybe long after they are gone.
- The wisest leaders don't hoard power. They build systems that outlive them, knowing that real leadership is measured by what happens after they leave.

　They don't need monuments.
They don't need credit.
　Their work speaks for itself.

What Will Your Fragrance Be?

At the end of your life, you won't care about how much money you made.
　You won't care about the awards, the promotions, or the followers.
　You will ask yourself:

- Did I love deeply?
- Did I help others grow?
- Did I leave the world a little better than I found it?

　If the answer is yes, you have lived well.
　Because in the end, legacy isn't what you take with you.
　It's what you leave behind in others.
　The camphor burns. It disappears. But its fragrance stays.
　May your life be the same.

The End. Or Rather, The Beginning.

You don't have to wait until the end of your life to start thinking about legacy.

Every conversation, every act of kindness, every piece of knowledge you share—is part of what you're leaving behind.

Starting today, burn brightly. Give fully. Let go of the need to be remembered.

Because the paradox is this: The ones who don't seek legacy are the ones who leave the greatest one.

Just like camphor.

AFTERWORD

? The Final Lesson of Camphor

The greatest impact you will ever have will not come from the things you hold on to. It will come from the things you release.

At the end of life, no one remembers how many promotions you got. No one remembers your follower count. What they remember is how you made them feel, the wisdom you shared, the lessons you left behind.

Camphor teaches us that the most powerful things in life are not those that remain, but those that transform.

So go. Burn completely. Give freely. Let go without fear.

Because the paradox of true power is this: the more you let go, the more you have.

?Notes & Further Reading (Optional, If You Want to Add More Depth)

If you're interested in exploring some of the ideas from this book in greater depth, here are some books, texts, and concepts that inspired Be Like Camphor:

1. Bhagavad Gita – The wisdom of detachment and karma yoga.
2. Tao Te Ching by Lao Tzu – The philosophy of effortless influence.
3. The Almanack of Naval Ravikant by Eric Jorgenson – The power of long-term thinking.
4. The Courage to Be Disliked by Ichiro Kishimi & Fumitake Koga – How detachment leads to freedom.
5. The Subtle Art of Not Giving a F*ck by Mark Manson – The paradox of true happiness.

These texts shaped my thinking, and I hope they do the same for you.

Final Thought

This book is complete.

But the real work begins now.

How will you choose to burn?

? Let go. Give fully. Leave a fragrance that lasts.